Contents

Glossary

On the last page, there is a glossary
of words and terms.
The glossary words appear
in **bold** in the text.

3

Who were knights?

Knights were tough, brave FIGHTING MEN who lived in the Middle Ages, or medieval times, from around A.D. 500 to A.D. 1500. They promised to fight loyally for kings and **lords**. In return, they were given land, treasures, and castles.

It took years to train to become a knight. At eight years old, boys went to live with a knight's family. They worked as **pages**.

At 14, they began work as **squires**. They learned how to fight, looked after the knight's horses, and helped him get ready for battle.

At 21, squires became knights in a special ceremony called dubbing.

A queen and knight in a dubbing ceremony.

The squire knelt in front of a king, queen, or lord, who tapped him on the shoulder with a sword and said, "Arise, Sir Knight."

The life of a knight

Knights hoped their **FAME** as fighters would live on after their deaths.

Knights were supposed to be **CHIVALROUS**—respectful and polite, especially to women.

Knights were supposed to **PROTECT** the **Christian religion**.

5

War on horseback

Knights fought on horseback, riding splendid warhorses called **DESTRIERS**. They were specially bred to be strong, fast, and obedient. Destriers were often very fierce and would kick and bite their knight's enemies.

A good warhorse was very expensive. It cost as much as a new car does today. Rich knights took two horses with them in battle, in case one was killed or injured.

Knights used teams of **packhorses** to carry bags of weapons and armor and carthorses to pull wagons filled with loot won in battle.

Only very wealthy knights could afford armor for their horses.

Riding a warhorse

Knights **STEERED** their horses using leather reins attached to a bit (a metal bar placed inside a horse's mouth).

METAL SPURS were attached to the heels of a knight's shoes. He pressed them against the horse's side to make it run faster.

Weapons and armor

Knights used long swords with very sharp edges for slashing at their enemies and short pointed swords for stabbing them through their armor. They also carried daggers **FOR SLITTING ENEMY THROATS.**

Knights hit out at their enemies with **maces**, **war hammers**, and battle-axes. They fended off enemy blows with wooden and metal shields.

A knight on horseback carrying a mace

Swords from medieval times

At first, knights wore padded leather **jerkins** covered by **chain-mail** tunics for protection.

A chain-mail tunic

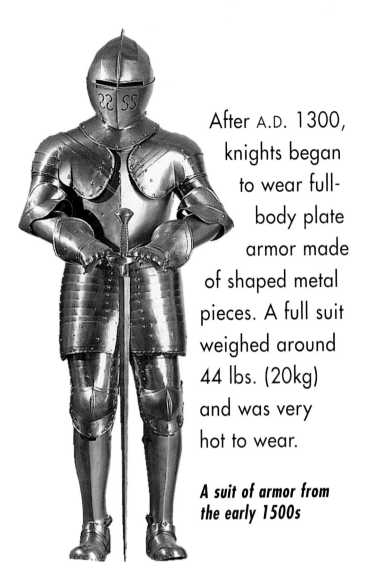

After A.D. 1300, knights began to wear full-body plate armor made of shaped metal pieces. A full suit weighed around 44 lbs. (20kg) and was very hot to wear.

A suit of armor from the early 1500s

Knights displayed **coats of arms** on their shields or armor to help identify themselves.

In the Middle Ages, records like this were kept, showing each noble family's coat of arms.

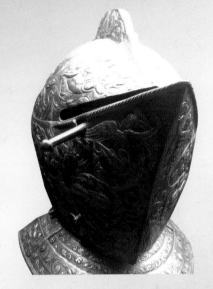

Knights wore protective HELMETS. They looked out through a movable piece called a visor.

Knights wore metal gloves called GAUNTLETS to protect their hands.

Charge!

At the start of a battle, knights on horseback stood side by side, in rows, facing the enemy. Then, suddenly, they CHARGED forward at top speed, bellowing fierce war cries.

This is a battle scene from the **Bayeux tapestry**, a huge piece of medieval embroidery.

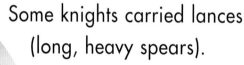

The Bayeux tapestry

A knight fights with a lance and sword in a battle scene from a movie.

Some knights carried lances (long, heavy spears). Lances could be used to knock an enemy off his horse. A knight on the ground was easier to attack. He might also get trampled by the horses!

Ordinary soldiers fought on foot. They used **pikes** to stab at knights and shot at them with longbows and crossbows.

Longbowmen shoot at a knight.

A skilled longbowman could shoot ten arrows every minute and hit targets 1,000 ft. (300m) away.

Medieval artifacts

LONGBOWS were made of yew wood. The arrows had metal tips.

Crossbows fired metal bolts that **SMASHED** through armor.

This metal spike is called a **CALTROP**. Caltrops were scattered in front of knights' horses to stab their hooves and make them fall.

11

Fighting for fun

During peacetime, knights fought **PRETEND BATTLES** with blunt (dull) weapons. These competitions were called jousts or tournaments. They helped knights practice their skills. Kings, queens, lords, and ladies all came to watch.

In a joust, two knights charged toward each other on horseback. The goal of the joust was to knock your opponent to the ground using a wooden lance.

During pretend battles, knights wore surcoats (robes) over their armor. They decorated them with their family coats of arms.

Modern-day actors reenact a medieval jousting competition.

Knights who lost a competition had to give their horses and armor to the winners. Some knights who were good at fighting became very rich this way!

Medieval artifacts

Ladies gave **LOVE TOKENS**, such as flowers, to their favorite fighters.

Knights topped their helmets with amazing crests shaped like birds or monsters.

Knights and spectators sheltered in colorful tents at jousts.

13

The first castles

Castles were the biggest, STRONGEST BUILDINGS around during the Middle Ages. They were safe forts where soldiers sheltered from enemies in wartime. Castles were also splendid homes for rich and powerful kings, lords, and knights.

The first castles were built around A.D. 900. They were wooden towers called **keeps**. After A.D. 1050, castle builders heaped up soil to make steep hills called mottes and also built wooden keeps on top.

In later times, keeps were built of stone.

A strong wooden fence was built around the motte. The area inside the fence was called a **bailey**. Soldiers in the castle used the bailey for keeping their warhorses safe and for storing food supplies.

You can see a motte-and-bailey castle in this section of the Bayeux tapestry.

This stone keep at York Castle, England, replaced the original wooden one.

Early fortifications

From around 800 B.C. to A.D. 200, the **Celts** built tall stone towers in Scotland called BROCHS.

Early castles and forts were built using simple tools and a lot of MUSCLE POWER. There were no power tools or big machines.

Towers and dungeons

After A.D. 1000, castles were built of stone. They had **HUGE** stone keeps, surrounded by high stone walls.

Castle walls were 3 ft. (1m) thick—or more. They were made of soil and stone rubble pounded together and covered with strong stone blocks on both sides.

Rocks were dropped on enemies from holes called machicolations.

Narrow slits for shooting arrows

This is Beaumaris Castle in Wales.

Castles were surrounded by a moat, a deep water-filled ditch. It could be crossed only by a drawbridge, which could be pulled up.

Castles were often used as prisons. Some had damp underground dungeons.

This picture shows a portcullis. It could be dropped quickly to stop **ENEMIES** from entering the main castle door.

The keep

Stone walls topped by battlements and walkways

Narrow spiral stone staircases inside towers made it difficult for **ATTACKERS** to use their swords.

Small towers made the walls stronger. They were used as lookout posts.

Under attack!

Enemies tried to capture castles in many different ways. Sometimes they dug holes under castle walls to make them fall down. Often they CRASHED into the castle gates with **battering rams**.

Attacking armies also besieged (surrounded) castles. They camped close by and blocked all the roads. They poisoned wells and streams and stopped all fresh food and water from reaching the people inside.

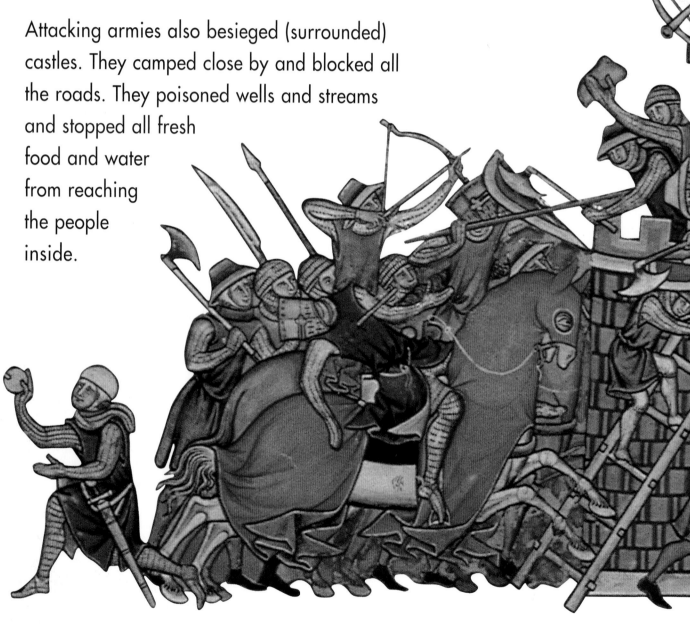

Some attackers hurled dead bodies over the castle walls in order to terrorize the people inside and spread disease.

People trapped inside a castle under **siege** had two choices—surrender and probably be killed or starve and die!

Castle defenders fought back, throwing stones and spears. One trick was to drop red-hot sand onto the attackers' heads.

Medieval warfare

This picture shows a trebuchet. It was used to SHOOT ROCKS over castle walls.

Defenders SHOT ARROWS at their attackers.

If a castle was captured, the **captain of the guard** had to hand over the keys.

Castle fun

When not at war, kings, lords, knights, and their families liked to have fun. They invited friends and important visitors to their castles and entertained them with **FEASTS, MUSIC, AND DANCING.**

Lords, knights, and noble ladies rode out to meadows with tame hawks. The hawks were trained to catch rabbits and small birds and then bring them back to their handlers.

A medieval painting of ladies on horseback

A hawk

Knights loved to go hunting for deer and wild boars in the woods. They hunted on horseback with fierce hunting dogs.

A statue in a beautiful castle garden

Many castles had gardens with fountains, fruit trees, and flowers. Noble ladies liked to spend time there, listening to **minstrels** singing love songs and reciting poetry.

Castle life

In the Middle Ages, people ate using their FINGERS, spoons, and knives. Forks were not normally used.

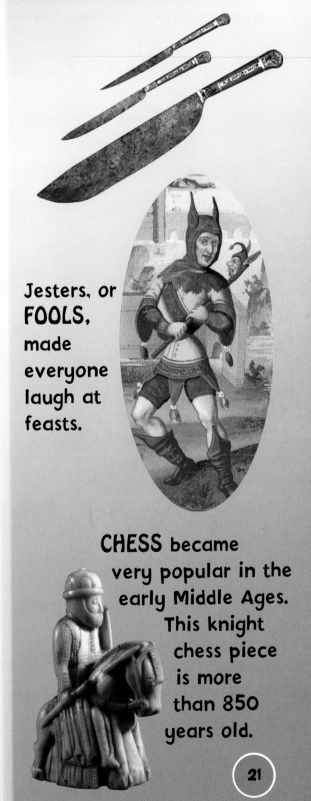

Jesters, or FOOLS, made everyone laugh at feasts.

CHESS became very popular in the early Middle Ages. This knight chess piece is more than 850 years old.

Knights and castles today

From around A.D. 1400, castles came UNDER ATTACK from new weapons called cannon. These enormous metal tubes were filled with gunpowder. They fired huge stone cannonballs, which had the power to smash down castle walls.

In 1460, King James II of Scotland was killed when his own new cannon exploded. He was showing his wife how it worked during the siege of Roxburgh Castle.

A cannon with cannonballs

By the end of the Middle Ages, kings, lords, and knights wanted stylish, comfortable houses to live in, and many castles fell into ruin.

Warwick Castle in England

Today, millions of tourists visit castle ruins throughout Europe every year.

Often, visitors to castles can watch exciting displays where actors reenact battles between medieval knights.

Castle myths

Since the Middle Ages ended, many myths have developed about castles.

Some people believe that they have seen **GHOSTS** in spooky castle corridors like this!

Fairy tales, such as **SLEEPING BEAUTY**, have been inspired by ruined castles in France.

23

Glossary

BAILEY A courtyard, surrounded by a wooden fence, outside a castle on a motte (mound of soil).

BATTERING RAMS Huge, heavy tree trunks used to smash castle walls and gates.

BAYEUX TAPESTRY An embroidered wall hanging. It is around 230 ft. (70m) long and shows the Norman (French) conquest of England in A.D. 1066.

CAPTAIN OF THE GUARD The officer in charge of soldiers guarding a castle.

CELTS People who were powerful in Europe from around 800 B.C. to A.D. 200.

CHAIN MAIL Armor made of thousands of small metal rings linked together.

CHRISTIAN RELIGION The faith of people who worship Jesus Christ.

COATS OF ARMS Special designs shown on shields, flags, badges, and armor. They were a sign of high rank (your position and importance in society).

JERKINS Jackets without collars or sleeves.

KEEPS The strong central towers of castles.

LORDS High-ranking men who owned land. They had to be loyal to kings. Knights and ordinary people had to be loyal to lords.

MACES Spiked metal balls on sticks. They were used as weapons.

MINSTRELS People who sang and played musical instruments as their job.

PACKHORSES Horses used for carrying heavy loads.

PAGES Young boys learning how to be squires. They worked as messengers for knights.

PIKES Deadly weapons—sharp spikes on long poles.

SIEGE An attack on a castle (or walled city). Enemies surrounded the castle. Then they tried to break through the walls or waited for the people inside to starve.

SQUIRES Teenage boys training to become knights. They learned fighting skills and how to ride horses.

WAR HAMMERS Heavy hammers made of metal. They were used as weapons.

Index